The Poetry Book

COMPLETE COLLECTION

Written by

AJ Kunkel

The Poetry Book

COMPLETE COLLECTION

FOR MORE INFORMATION VISIT
WWW.AJKUNKEL.COM

Volumes 1 – 4

Trust Your Instincts
&
Chase Your Dreams

- AJK

Volume 1

Uno

They say the number
One
Is the loneliest
Of them all
That when you are alone
You are bound
To fall
But I've learned
To be on my own
Me, myself, and I
The
Only true people I've ever
Known
Nothing is ever
Set in stone
No man can ever
Be fully-grown
We are learning
Everyday
The weak bow down
As
The brave conquer the grey
In the end
What will the next generation say
Of what we've done
On this day
You can choose
To feel afraid
To see your dream
Fade
Or you can strive
Into the unknown
With the skin on your back
And
The strength in your bone

Lovers

The feeling resides within
One hundred fifty pounds of sin
Your fingers soothing my skin
Lips pressed up against your chin
Good might lose
Evil may win
The intensity flourishes
This drug called love
Nourishes
My soul
Replacing what the devil stole
Breathe...
Stay under control
Fall into my eyes
No more games
No more lies
We are what we both
Despise
From the lazy to the wise
We shall all meet our demise
Inhale this toxic fume
Wake up in this shadowy room
For today is our day
And tomorrow our doom

Home Less

Deception knows all
Yet we still create a wall
Help needed
And God Bless
What if this was a test
Are we good
Do we do what we should
We pass by everyday
A hungry mouth with nothing to say
If God were in front of you
Would you obey
Creating your own reality
A story with no formality
Talk is cheap
Taking action is deep
Kindness is sweet
Spare some shoes
For the cold feet
In the end what really matters
The daily gossip and city chatters
No
Forgiveness and gratitude
Peacefulness to end any feud
Innocence to wash away the crude
We are all the same
Growing up hoping for fame
Most just holding a pound of shame
Some are broken
Some you cannot explain
Everyone falls
Some harder than others
But in the end of things
We are all sisters and brothers

The Howling Moon

Emerging from the water
Head going numb
Body growing hotter
Clothes I once worn
Now torn
Pulling myself to shore
Pistol on my hip
Don't know what for
Howls of the night grow loud
Young wolves
Looking to make their father's proud
Fear setting in now
Fresh river water
Dripping from my brow
Insanity a possible concern
Fingertips begin to burn
Notice movement near the fern
Thoughts of the end
My mind begins to bend
Heart triggers
The veins send
Blood rushing to my core
What could be in store
From the rich to the poor
A man is the same
Courage mixed with shame
Walk steady and strong
This could be wrong
Hearing the same old song
Boom
Bang
In this field I awake
Half past noon
Thus is the curse of the howling moon

Colt 45

Out here
It would appear
That one should give into fear
The year is 1877
I just turned eleven
Father is out back
My brother is with him
His name is jack
Mother is preparing supper
Honey would you please close the shudder
Yes yes mam I say with a stutter
Kids at school mutter
About me under their breath
Something is stirring
Talk in the town
Of a man named death
Lightning and thunder roar
Just outside the front door
A man walks closer to the house
Calm like the wind
Silent like a mouse
He steps inside
I can now hear him breathing
In the place where I reside
I step out of my bed
He begins to listen
Then turns his head
I pick my tool up
And fill it with lead
Soon one will live
And one shall be dead
The man enters my room
Looking to hand me my doom
Feeling afraid yet finally alive
I pull the trigger
Of my Colt 45

The Obsessive Man

Check the wallet three times
Two twenties
And four dimes
Driver license and credit card
Left wrist still freshly scarred
He repeats to himself
No regard for his health
Can still hear the alarms ringing
Sounds of people screaming
$250,000 in the passenger seat
Life beginning to feel complete
Start the car
Strike a match
Inhale this black tar
Look to the left
Look to the right
One cop and three cars in sight
Release the emergency brake
Hands begin to shake
Mind wanders
Begins to worry
Vision becoming blurry
Place the car in reverse
Eyesight growing worse
Feeling as if he's driving his own hearse
Hands still stable
As if he was able, to stop time
And erase the memory
Of ever committing the crime
Sirens not far behind now
Prays and says his vow
As he starts to accelerate
He begins to accept his fate
Though it may be too late
He repeats the one thing he still believes
"There's no honor among thieves."

Noir

Grey whiskey on a Sunday morning
Devil will take you without warning
Cigarettes till midnight
Read the Bible to shed new light
If happiness is what I seek
Yet
Darkness overtakes the weak
No wonder my future
Looks so bleak
Dim lit alleyways
Murder, Theft, Gangs
Consumes most of my days
Fathers raising their sons
Blood dripping from their tommy guns
Hardest job in the city
To take care of the hopeless
And ones with no pity
Good against evil
This towns gone medieval
Every day is the same
New victim
With no name
It's starting to become a game
Us versus them
Children, women, men
They'll slaughter any in their path
Stay out of their way
Or you might fall in their wrath
But there is hope
I am writing this to the man himself
To the man who kills, to create his own wealth
So don't misunderstand my tone
I will defeat you
Mr. Al Capone

Sticks and Stones

She said, he said, they said
Gossip the oldest disease to spread
Leaving more dead
Then any other crime around
And just cause it doesn't sound
Like anything that'll hurt someone
It's the opposite of fun
It could all end
With the firing of a gun
Rumors
Are like tumors
They can destroy an innocent life
Slip and a slice
With that pretty looking knife
Bullies put others down
Hurt
A four-letter noun
Yeah but it's a noun that sticks
The insecure give into
The devil's tricks
So maybe we should change
Go from normal to strange
Show others love
Shout out to the big man above
But when push comes to shove
People break
Hands begin to shake
Minds become an earthquake
Next morning they may never wake
Love and peace
Lets have a decrease in hate
A little less debate
Hopefully at this rate
We will sit and wait
For an answer to the mystery
Of our Hateful History

Graduation

Wake up breathing heavy
Anxiety filling up
Like water breaking a levee
Reach over to my right
Time
3:40 at night
Open the yearbook
Taking a look
At the old days
The old me, and my old ways
Classic smile
With laced up J's
To think
I was unhappy back then
Writing poetry
With my brown colored pen
Grass isn't greener on the other side
So maybe my teachers
Never lied
I was that kid
Complaining about what others did
Always judging people
Then going off
And praying at the church steeple
Sometimes I am not who I appear
Just a captain of a sinking ship
Trying to steer
Never got to say
My dear
Love never entered the equation
My mind has become
My own nation
I need to stop
Regretting who I was
Before my graduation

Fell in Love with the wrong girl

External
Paternal
Eternal
Words flowing through
This journal
At this age
I can turn the page
Step onto a new stage
Make myself into anything
Yeah
But I've tried everything
Even tried to sing
Took a chance in the ring
Wasn't my thing
Stuck now
Wondering how
It could be
That you and me
Are so distant
Yet
You were the one being persistent
On us being together
Loves like a feather
Floats great
Until it hits bad weather
I say
Aren't we in this together
Loosening this tether
Simple seduction
Is stranger than fiction
Must be this drug addiction
Making me feel this affliction
My only prediction
Is that you
Will always be my conviction

Cowboy

There once was a man long ago
Who knew about the evil ones
And a thought came into his head
A thought that could end up with him dead
But he didn't care
He sat down in his old rocking chair
Why be bad
When it just makes others sad
And in that very second
He prepared for his revival
Realizing it was his job
To reverse the cycle
Too switch from sad to glad
He said to himself
"My name is D.R. Roy"
And it's my destiny to be a cowboy
So he holstered his gun
Blazing a new trail
Under the broken sun
Now devoted to cleansing the evil off this earth
Finally finding some self worth
Striking the earthly demons down everyday
There was no time to play
Within this land of sinners and saints
He controls who paints
With the blood of their enemies and foes
He controlled the yes's and the no's
This power began to overtake him
He felt as if he was drowning
Yet still able to swim
Future now looking dim
Day by day evil began to grow stronger
He couldn't stop it any longer
"Had the evil ones really prevailed?"
He said to himself
Forgetting the past

He grabbed his gun off the shelf
Not for the soft hearted
He went off to finish what he had started
Weak and frail
The man finished off the earthly demons
One by one
Through the night
And until he saw the sun
Walking back into town
He saw a child kneeling on the ground
He asked the child what was wrong
The child replied
"What's taken you so long?"
As the child stood up
The man asked the boy
What he wanted to be when he grew up
The child stared into the mans eyes
Holstered his toy
And replied
"I'm going to be a cowboy."

1995 – Infinity

Death
Just a five-letter phrase
Yet
Can ruin us for days
Letting it grab ahold of our minds
Trapping us
Feeling confined
But it's just a word
Rest be assured
Everyone shall pass
So why waste time
With that liquid filled glass
It isn't bringing you anywhere
Got addicted
In a game of truth or dare
Oh
You're caught in the snare
Of how to act
What to wear
Who to be
And how to swear
Youth these days
Stuck in this generations maze
Hypnotized by sins gaze
Eyes glossy from this weekly daze
No time to fail
Building my ship
Preparing to sail
Away from here
To a land with no fear

Seven–Eleven

Summer midnights
Electric feelings with no lights
Parking lot fights
Should I get a slurpee
Or
Maybe
Even the Arizona iced tea
Or the 60-second burrito
Possibly the sat all day taquito
An e cig
With a side
Of fig
Newtons
Pack of tortillas
But I need to watch my gluten
Pack of American spirits
Lets reach our inner Rasputin
Nights like these
Young middle of the night breeze
Moments we were meant to seize
No thinking
Just time to breathe
Ask for forgiveness later
The jealous
Is just the opposite of a hater
See that girl
I would date her
Cheap pick up lines
Parking ticket, illegal substance, Public indecency
Fines
Wine and dines
Are for the old peeps
For the grandmas and the creeps
Lets have a little more truth
And a little
Less bleeps

Oblivious Girl

Once knew a girl
Pretty in pink
More expensive than a pearl
Wanted everything
But the world
Father left her
When she was young
Sexuality
The song she sung
Seduction
The bell she rung
Hurt
The word with what she stung from
I knew a little bit
About this one
Knew she was fun
But
Threw away every guy
When she was done
With him
No compassion
But equipped with style
And a sense for fashion
Won the heart of every man
Ten dollar
Cheap spray tan
Thought she owned the earth
Tricked the wrong man
Then realized self worth
It was too late
She had sealed
Her fate
She would be alone
For the rest of her life
At this rate

Secret Cigarettes

Bella
The youngest of them all
Had a
Mind of a rebel
Yet the
Face of a doll
Three sisters
One brother
And an
Absent mother
Life had been rough
Learned how to be tough
Stood up straight
And
Could call any man's bluff
No one knew
But only a few
Of sweet Bella's
Secret vice
No one would've
Thought twice
Of how she
Rolled the dice
Betting the ultimate price
Her life
She didn't care
Life wasn't fair
Blonde looking
Smokey smelling
Hair
Five a day
Twenty in the tray
Thirty-five packs
A week
Future looked promising
Now looking bleak

Private School Kids

Sit up straight
Comb your hair
Make sure not to be late
Teachers always right
No need for debate
No control over one's fate
Have to be over 18
To date
Only white undershirts
Principal measured skirts
Poor girls turned away
No need for any more flirts
Must get good grades
Oh you
Made a mess
Call over the maids
Spoon fed children
Firmly hold the pen
Believe nothing but the truth
Classy Looking
Youth
Never trust anyone
Sitting alone
In a corner booth
Now graduated and free
Everyone saying
Be who you want to be
Yeah
But seriously
Who's me
Never made my own decisions
Other adults
In separate divisions
In life
Now making
Multiple revisions

Unemployed after High School

Currently 10:09
Writing this
Actually feeling fine
Quit my job five
Days ago
Thinking of teaching
Myself how to sew
Probably should go out
And make some dough
Bills piling up
Kool-Aid rising
In my cup
Demons of failure
Saying sup
Parents ask me if I'm a loser
I say yup
Tripping on my past
Wanting to break something
Maybe drive my car really fast
Am I in cast away
What have I done all day
11:22
Bored out of my mind
Hoping for the flu
Nothing to do
Write some poetry
Eat some glue
Talk to myself
What's up
Oh nothing new
Now officially losing it
Press play
Then pause
Screw it
I'll just sit here
Watching jaws

Catchy pick up lines

This poem will be about the cute stuff
Have you been lifting
You're looking pretty buff
If I was a pirate ship
I would bite your bottom lip
Are you from another universe
Because you're making my radioactive spider bite feel worse
If you were in a hearse
I would definitely be your nurse
Are you from the Jersey Shore
Cause you're making me feel poor
If I wrote poems for the hell of it
Would you teach me how to knit
I'm kind of a sort of a hipster
Would you like to play twister
You remind me of my mom
And my neighbor across the street Tom
If I was a bird in a tree
I would hope you could scream like a banshee
I really hope you take these to heart
They can be the start
To a wonderful relationship
Like salsa
To a beautifully crafted tortilla chip
One last
Line
The best of them all
If you didn't know how to walk
I would learn how to crawl

19th Poem

Wow
I actually made it this far
Still trying to find money
To pay for my car
I used to play golf
Once shot 3 under par
Enough about me
Thanks for paying the fee
To listen to the words from my soul
Just thought about
A fishing pole
Ok
For the rest of this poetry
I'll rhyme about the sea
It's so blue
It makes me want to pee
And the sand is free
Literally
It doesn't cost money
Bee's also make honey
Wait
That was distracting
Did you know I used to be
Into acting
Why are you still reading this
I really need to
Never mind
How did you even find
This crappy book of randomness
Just punched a wall
WITH MY FIST
Driving to the hospital
I guess I broke my wrist
Ok well it's been fun
I'm seriously done
With this

For No Reason

Bullets appearing
Court hearings
Lip piercings
Rebellious
Business of radicals
Two-year sabbaticals
Puppet friends
Lincoln and Wilkes Booth
Make amends
The C word
Offends
Sarcastic fashion trends
Double Cheeseburger
With extra
Sugar
Diamond covered Luger
Alright I've had
Enough of this nonsense
Time to recompense
You all
It's the season
To have no reason
I may have
Just committed
Poetry treason
But
Forgive
A young man like thee
Plant a seed
Work hard
And succeed like me
Do what you love
And love what you do
There are many who listen
But
Few who tie my shoe

Video Games

Probably should stop and eat
Or else my energy will deplete
Sitting here
Where are my feet
Haven't gotten out of bed
If I leave
My character will end up dead
Enough said
Bring me some water
And
A side of bread
Reload
The lead
Never stop playing
Till I lose
Consciousness in my brain
Controlling life one point at a time
Currently not working
Not making a dime
Locked away in this house
Staying away from crime
Parents
Making my steak
To the prime
Optimist
Looking at a pessimistic
Lifestyle
Haven't seen the sun in a while
Probably
Should get outside
And run a mile
But for now
I'll just
Load this saved game file

Yours truly,

Beginning from the start
I stared at this blank paper
Then it naturally became art
Didn't choose to write
Didn't choose to create poems
Hours past midnight
First one written
On the red eye flight
From New York City
While in high school
I believed I deserved pity
But that was gritty
Of me to think
Selfishness consumed me
While others cried bent over the sink
Sure
I may have reached the brink
Maybe had a little too much to drink
But life wasn't that bad
And there I was
Feeling sad
For myself
Putting my dreams
On the shelf
Waiting for other people to rescue me
When the only
Person that could help
Was thee
So now I speak with purpose
Leaving the haters
Wordless
We each have a reason
For being on this planet
Though it may take time to foresee
I wish you all the best of luck
Yours truly,

Rap Music

Used to make rap music
Then stopped
Like a nerve ending popped
Wasn't like that though
Always dreamed of rapping
At my own show
Never did make a dime
Yet I
Still know how to rhyme
And that's something
That can't be taught
Once started
Can't even be stopped
Like a blood clot
Everybody else
Was just talk
Rapping about girls and pot
While I use my gift
To lift
And inspire
While I create my empire
On the daily
Facing the fire
While you smoke out
And get higher
I'll pay my dues
So you can call me your sire
Think I'm a liar
That's fine
Just sit there and whine
Cut yourself
On this thorn filled vine
Complain how life isn't fair
It's because you hooligans
Never learned to dare
I've forgotten about you, you're out of my care

Heaven and Hell

What's after this
Wooden coffins
Floating into the mist
Who will be on the eternal list
Whether it was an accident
Or that slice on your wrist
We'll all be there
Fighting what's fair
No man can run
From deaths snare
Whether by his own doing
Or an electric chair
We shall all see the day
Where he will say
The spoken truth
Sins of our
Youth
Knees bent
Repent
Now
And thee shall be forgiven
From the good to the wicked
We were all
Once driven
Reality is just an illusion
The perfume
To instill our sinful confusion
Nearing the end times
Climaxing towards a conclusion
Non-believers to believers
To and fro
Believe what you must
But in the end
Where will you go

Birth Day

Can you remember
Your first memory
Your first taste of dairy
First feeling
That was scary
The moment you believed
Your tooth had been
Taken by a fairy
First time you thought about
Who you were going too marry
This journey we are
All on
Is like the sunset
To a midnight dawn
One second we are here
In
One moment we will be gone
Our time is fragile
The decisions we gamble
We are all
Able to achieve greatness
So whether
You are mopping the floor
Or sitting
And hoping for more
We each
Have a destiny
And
Shall walk through that door
For
One day
We shall all know
What we are here for

Carnival

Cue the 1950's tunes
Throw the dart
Pop the balloons
First kiss behind
The merry go round
Hearing the moment
Smelling the sound
Around and around
We go
Walk fast
Then slow
One day I'll build us
A chateau
And a fireplace
For when we get snow
Cotton candy
Like pink whipped cream
Are you understanding
This radical theme
Meet the legend
Who chose to walk up stream
While everyone gave in
See this scar
On my chin
Yeah
But I still have this
Great old grin
Can't let the world
Put you down son
They haven't won
A real man never
Chooses to run
But faces the monster within
With his great
Old grin

Blue Eyed Mermaid

Crisp and clear
The lagoon is inviting
Moon rises
Perfect lighting
Waves beyond the ocean
Something is stirring
Causing a commotion
Her face rises from the water
Sailor's eyes gazing
Upon the foreign creature
They call upon
The preacher
He sees the unknown
His hands and feet
Turn to stone
The creature rises fully from
The sea
Full length
7ft 3
Fear entering the ship
Captain pours some rum
Takes another sip
Alright men
We only have one shot
When I count to ten
Fire everything we got
The creature grew closer
As the captain and his crew
Aimed at the speeding dot
The captain turned to his shipmates
It's either her
Or we rot
The pirates threw over a net
And there she was caught
No time to be afraid
Thus is the tale of the Blue Eyed Mermaid

Now or Never

Do you believe
In fate
Or is it too
Late
To understand your place
Sometimes
In life
What we face
Things that are not
Safe
Things that threaten
Our well being
Constrain rather than freeing
Blind us
From ever seeing
The truth of our path
Cleanse our minds
Take a bath
The time is now
The moment to vow
To seek how
We
Must create something new
Lay down
Or
Pull through
The agonizing fire
Aspire
To be the inspiration
Behind the choir
Whatever you imagine
Can transpire
Into reality
Stay clever
For today
It's now or never

Your Moment

Inspiration
The most powerful
Sensation
So here's the choice
When you feel
Loud enough
To spread your voice
I dare
Each and every one of you
To achieve something
You never thought you could do
Strive for things
Build your wings
Take flight
Into the daunting
Night
Push through the darkness
And into the light
Because we each
Have the right
To make something
Out of our lives
It's your moment
Own
It
Show the haters
And debaters
That you won't break
For heavens sake
You only have one life
So fight
And live it right

Volume 2

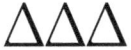

Haunted Mansions

Here we stand
Underneath the fame
Bullets like rain
She tells me my lips
Take away the pain
To her own gain
I feel the shame
This world plays us
Like some sick game
The clouds feel low
The devil has always been my foe
Water falls to see life grow
This liquid hides my tears
Sounds of thunder
Disguises my fears
Part of this generation
That has no aspiration
Just clones, aspiring towards
Likes on their phones
Hearing the
Shallow ghosts
Moans
Down the hallway
In this mansion
Up in my head

Strapped to this bed
I'm alive
Which is the opposite
Of being dead
Yet instead
Of living
I'm regretting
Stupidly letting
The here and now
Go to waste
My overthinking
Is based
On an Idea of
Nonsense
Something hollow
Nothing dense

Writers Block

Where is the key
To this lock
That causes
Wait what was it
Oh yeah
Writers block
Literally sitting here
For hours
Dipping my hand
In some slime
Now got super powers
There and back
Lost a bet
Cue the smoke
And the 1970's
Jet
Feel this freedom
Let go
Of your regret
Not ready to give up
Yet
Still have demons
To face

Taking my time
In this lifetime
Of a race
Here I am
POOF!
Then gone
Without a trace
You can all be
The first astronaut
In your own
Personal space
Just always
Promote peace
With a healthy
Side of grace

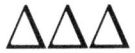

The Coldest

Frost melts
As
The sun appears
Over the trees
Within perfect harmony
The birds and the bees
Soar through the air
Within minutes
Flowers begin rising
Through the earth's
Vulnerable tears
Emerging from the forest
After a long
Slumber
With glossy eyes
And a heavy stare
Two cubs
And
A momma bear
White snow
Evaporates with the sun's glow
Green textures
Arise
Like a single truth
Forcing it's way through

A million lies
When one lives
Another dies
When one laughs
Another cries
When one gives up
Another tries
Life may feel cold
Tired and old
While others feel
Young and bold
You see life is made up of seasons
For every ten questions
There will always be a thousand reasons
For every war
There will only be a handful of treasons
Sometimes we feel as if we are
At our warmest temperature
And other times
Our coldest
The cold either makes
Us or breaks us
But
We must decide for ourselves
Who we will each become
In
The coldest

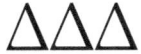

While Waiting In Line

In the back of the line
Drinking some soda
Feeling pretty fine
The sun is out
Sounds of a roller coaster
And a child's shout
This boredom
Forces me to doubt
What this thing called
Life is really about
Are we supposed to succeed
Or simply perform one good deed
A day away now
Holy Cow!
This line really needs to move
Right
About
Now
Frustration I can feel it
Patience I can't deal with it
Feeling sorry for myself
Wishing I had a better life
A girl, more money, a cooler car
Then suddenly I see from afar
A young boy

Smiling brighter than any star
Trying to sit in the
Roller coaster car
His eyes are filled with joy
His mother hands him
His favorite Buzz Lightyear toy
The ride begins to move
And with it the boy
Minutes passed by
Felt like forever
The boy returned from his ride
His smile still enormous and wide
The lap bar pulls up
I wait to see him step out
And walk towards his parents
Yet instead I see something unfair
He's helped up into a gray wheelchair
He's paralyzed from the waist down
Yet he still smiles
Never showing a frown
And here I am complaining about
Money, people, and my career
While that young boy has already
Conquered fear
He never questions when things
Seem unclear
Or worries about some silly old career
He smiles and laughs
In the moments that are given
I mean he is really living
Life
The right way
That boy in the wheelchair
Who really did shine
Taught me so much
While waiting in line

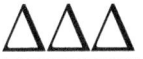

Kissing You Before Midnight

Our hands
Interlocking
On command
So natural
Yet
Beautifully unique
Looking into my eyes
I kiss you on the cheek
You carry me
When I'm weak
They say we're just
Young
That it's the same song
They sung
That the fire
Will tire
Over time
Yet I still rhyme
Feeling sublime
These are the days
To never forget
So never let
Anyone pull you
Away
From me

Though I cannot
Foresee
What is to come
If I lost you
I would feel numb
This world has become
Sour
We have each other
For this final hour
In this moment
Embracing this power
Feelings begin
Taking flight
While I kiss you
Before midnight

ΔΔΔ

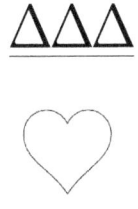

Tomorrow

If yesterday was today
Would you press pause
Or would you press play
I mean, we all say
"Oh I'll do it tomorrow or some other day"
But why not now
Not tomorrow
NOW
Punch fear in the face
BOOM! SLAM! POW!
The seconds we waste
Worrying about tomorrow
Creating false sorrow
Use the time you are given
Face your demons
And shout
I Am Driven!
To become something
Worth remembering
Begin Dismembering
Those negative feelings
Inside your head
Silence the uncontrollable dread
That leaves you paralyzed
While laying in bed

Right now you are alive not dead
So instead of taking the usual
Route that leads to doubt
Search for what life's all about
Stay calm, while others shout
Because life's too short
To be afraid or even doubt
That fire within your soul
Go chase that dream
Achieve that goal
'Cause in the end
Time isn't something you just borrow
It waits for no man
And it sure won't wait for tomorrow

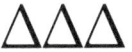

—————

Clockwork

April, May, June
Gears shifting
Starting up soon
The lonely man
Sits on the moon
Listening to the universe's
Tune
Everybody has somewhere
To be
Something else to see
Wouldn't you agree
Empty faces
And hearts
Drinking whiskey
And throwing darts
These bars
Full of emotion
This past year
I've committed to
Incredible devotion
Waiting for my
Promotion
Seems like everything
Flows like the ocean
Except for me

Wouldn't you agree
Now bent on
One knee
Hoping for a ticket
Out of here
Waiting for the
Final gear
To take it's
Place
In the final
Moments of this
Race
Faith in one hand
Negative choices
On which I stand
I am my own
Brand
Within this false land

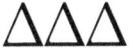

Sweet Heart

Unconditional
Feelings throughout
Underdogs
Estimating doubt
The one
I'm meant to fall for
Could be
Behind any door
Yet
I'm afraid to look
Rain falling
While I'm
Writing in this nook
Crafting my own
Book
Candle burning through
It's wick
Wearing a suit
Looking pretty slick
Confidence within
Is the trick
The party begins
Light dims
Slow motion intact
Beautiful people everywhere

To be exact
Love is in the air
I see her
She notices my stare
That special moment
We share
Then and there
I knew
Out of the 7 billion
There was nothing
I could do
She was the one meant for me
And I could tell
She would agree
Such a spontaneous
Start
For when I met
My sweet heart

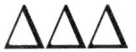

_____

Bus Stop

Winter, spring, summer
The fall
I'm only 73 inches
Tall
Sitting alone
Feeling out of sorts
Waiting for my transport
Out of here
My
Future
Still unclear
Yet the past
Has seemed to last
While moving along
Truth or False
I answered it wrong
Playing our song
In my mind
Always being kind
Turn the other cheek
Seek
No approval from
Others
Never hide from
The monster

Under your covers
In front of me
Lovers
Is all I see
But wasn't that
Supposed to be
You and me
I let you
Be free
Now regretting this
Squeezing my fist
Waiting for my
Gold watch
To appear on my wrist
Writing till I reach the top
Dreams growing
While I wait
At this bus stop

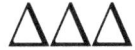

The Old Man In The Corner Booth

I saw an old man
Sitting alone in the corner booth
Behind him sat another man
Young
Bold
And strong
The young one
Had been on his phone
For much too long
The old man
Watched the birds and the bees
While the young man
Talked about
Money and new car keys
The old man stared
At the wind flowing through
The trees
While the young one
Focused on the I's and the ME's
The old man seemed content
While the young man
Yelled on his phone
Seemed like an argument

Time passed
It came
And it went
A true difference between ages
As if the older man
Was onto other pages
In some other book
Just by the way he would look
At everything
As if he knew something else
We didn't
Does knowledge come with age
Will I feel at peace
In the next stage
Of life
Well I cannot answer that
But if you are seeking some truth
Maybe you should go ask
The old man in the corner booth

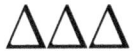

Empire of Regret

Kids exploring
Ignoring common sense
Coming up with
A pretense
One in particular
A kid lawless
Enough to search
For something new
Something else to do
Met a girl
She changed his world
Introduced him to
Everyone
Before this
He could only
Speak with his
Fist
He was finally
Alive
He could strive
Towards his goals
While holding her hand
On the morning
Strolls
Her eyes

Washed away
His tendency
To create lies
She was his everything
It was his reason
To move onto
The next season
She was always there
Her love
Was his only care
Though the day came
In which
She spoke
Of another name
This other man was now a threat
Thus created
The Empire of Regret

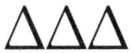

_____

Empire of Lust

So you're doing
Good
Standing where
The greats
Stood
Then the unexpected
Occurs
You grow up
Learn how
To spit new
Slurs
Therapy
Reassures
Yet temptation
Becomes the
Narration
Of your story
Dreaming
Of infinite glory
Television
Is now making
The decision
Crash collision
Up ahead
Yet

Forgetting what they
Said
Now ending up in
Bed
With someone
New every night
Oh
What a delight
Wait
Umm
Nope
Now you have
No hope
No true way
To cope
No one to hand you this rope
Heart turning into rust
AKA The Empire of Lust

ΔΔΔ

♡

PYRAMID

So
I am
No one
Important
Yet I have the
Ability to speak
In front of you now.
So "***who are you***" today

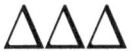

The Expectation of Yesterday

Day 1
Joyful laughter
Coming off as
Fun
While we're here
Let's run
Not stopping till
The fireworks
Are done
Multiple lands
To explore
From the mountains in space
To the
Pirates on the shore
Secrets behind
Every door
Pure good
No
Blood or gore
Heart warming
Within my core
I'm a young man
But within this
Land
I feel like a

Kid
As if the innocence
Never did
Leave my soul
Now it's out
Of my control
I'm happy
What a new creation
This concludes
The first day
Of my expectation

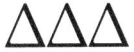

The Experience of Today

Woke up early
Today
Truly enjoying
My stay
Traveling from
The pirate's bay
Towards
The snow-covered mountain
Maybe throw
A penny or two
In the magical
Fountain
It granted
My wish
Now I see
Joyful mermaids
And
A
Talking fish
Got lost
Now haunted by
This mansion
Heard it's some
Sort of
Attraction

Saw my friends
While climbing this wall
Guess this
World is pretty
Small
Leaves are turning
Preparing to
Fall
All these
Kids trying to get in
Jumping the fence
This was my experience

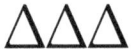

The Realization of Tomorrow

The squirrels here
Are free
To be
To roam
Because simply
This is their
Home
Joy
Saves
Today
I explored
Some caves
Made a splash
Created some new
Waves
Fought pirates
On the sand
Met a girl named
Alice
In a place
Called wonderland
Turns out
This place has
Its own band
This sure has been

Something grand
People change here
Or at
Least it would
Appear
That people forget
About their
Fear
And just
Focus on the
Good
Like we all
Should
A quiet concentration
Formed this
Timeless
Realization

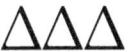

———————

<u>Young Wounds</u>

It was early
Not in time
But before I
Could rhyme
I could still
Love
And
So it began
As a young man
Searching for acceptance
In all the
Wrong corners
Of the earth
Comparing affection
To my own
Self worth
I had invested
In this
Self proclaimed lie
Why
Did I feel
As if
I needed another
To feel wanted
Oh

It's because everyone
Else simply
Flaunted
Their lover
In my face
My young face
Practically filled
With disgrace
But
We all grow up
Don't we
And to tell you the truth
I wouldn't be
Who I am today
If I hadn't
Experienced that pain
It's one thing to survive the storm
But another to dance in the rain

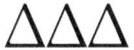

L.A.

L.A.
About 380 miles
From the
San Francisco Bay
Probably could make it
There
Within
A day
I was born here
And
Decided to stay
It's mostly sunny
But
Sometimes
Skies are gray
It's an adventure
Around here
A mysterious land
Shrouded in fear
You could disappear
Or
Start a career
It's the land
Where the ambitious
Persevere

Personalities
Ranging from
Liars
To the
Sincere
To me one
Thing has always
Been clear
I'll always gamble to win
So lets grab
The bottle
And spin

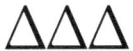

The Estate

This overgrown
Estate
Chooses my
Fate
Old power
Will not wait
For a young
Man
Like me
These walls
Restricting
Us from being
Free
Tall hedges
The color
Of money
Block the sun from me
Searching daily
I've been bred
To believe
In lies
And to not
Show emotion
When someone
Dies

My brother
Is punished
Whenever he
Cries
This land
Is hollow
This money
Is
Shallow
This life
For me
Stems from a seed
Of greed
I pray now
Never did before
Nothing to lose
Maybe it'll
Open a door

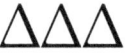

3014

One thousand
Years
From now
Robots
Serving a sadistic
Crowd
The ones made
Of flesh
Heavy and loud
Oh how
Lazy they've
Become
Thinking they
Have won
Metal gears
Turning
A new millennium
Burning
A revolution
Now stirring
Bones are made
For breaking
Heads now
Shaking
This world

Is theirs
For the taking
Metal against flesh
Now's the time
To express
The downward
Spiral
Swelling
This is the end
The metallic creature
Begins yelling
The
Time is now
For the flesh to bow
Silence now
Haunts
This
3014 crowd

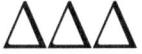

The Moon Landing

The atmosphere
Is near
So I threw a
Spear
I think it
Landed
Somewhere
Near my career
But
It hasn't begun
So
I guess
I'll have some
Fun
Yesterday
I touched the
Sun
Shooting stars
Flew past me
Like speeding
Cars
Took a nap
On
Mars
Trapped some

Meteors
In these honey jars
Space shuttle
Made of cardboard
Clouds
Formed this
Sword
Feet planted
Seven wishes granted
Now noticing
Where I'm standing
Just had
My own
Moon landing

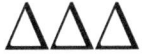

Shattered Mirrors

Windows
Clear windows
Outline this room
Rainfall stops
Then begins to
Resume
The earth's tears
Run across these
Hollow mirrors
Thunder roars
While the crowd
Cheers
Within each drop
I revisit my
Fears
All my trials
And
Failed careers
Now looking
Into these
Hollow mirrors
Once again
Place some ink
Into this rusty
Pen

I'm a writer
Always have been
Now it's not
If
But
When
You gain the
Courage to pursue
To do
What they said
Couldn't be done
You'll need to run
Prove them wrong
For the weak
Have to press on
Before they can become strong

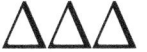

A N X I E T Y

How can I
Explain this
Think of a
Broken wrist
Like having one
Hand
And only
One fist
Now you're stuck
In a box
The walls are
Impenetrable
Just like cold
Rocks
You only
Have that broken
Wrist
To create a way
Out
And to see
The light of
Day
But inside that
Box it's
Dark and gray

You push every wall
And you call
And call
For a way
Out
People hear the yelling
But don't care
What it's all about
So you begin
To shout
You're hand is fully
Broken
So you take
Another route
Kicking the walls
But
Suddenly the ceiling
Falls

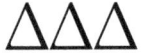

Real Eyes

Real eyes
Despise
The lies
The broken
Cries
The dreamers
Rise
The cheater
Tries
The abused
Puts on a
Disguise
The lazy
Go up in size
The lucky
Wins the prize
The unbeliever
Sighs
The believers
Baptize
The hopeless
Dies
The underdog
Flies
The evil

Will meet
Their demise
The good
Will float
Into the skies
So in the
End
We realize
That
To have
Real eyes
Means you are
Human
No one is perfect
We all make mistakes
We all mess up
But that's ok
Because we're human

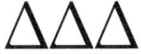

Flooded Thoughts

Too many items
On the
Checklist
These obstacles
Squeezing my
Fist
These reoccurring lines
On my wrist
The sins
Disappearing
Into the mist
My brain
Is
Flooded
With
Thoughts
Like a tangled rope
With
Ten thousand knots
Sitting down
Now
Breathing carefully
Focusing
On my
Legacy

Mentally
Preparing my soul
For the
Control
Needed to achieve
This dream
That to others
May seem
Impossible
But to
Me
I see
A way out
And
In the end
Isn't that what
Life's all
About

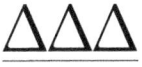

These Moments

It's hard to find
Real people these days
Everyone's caught up
In their old ways
Trapped within this world's maze
Staring at the sun
Eyes stuck within it's daze
Let me rephrase
Something that I've been trying
To say these past few days
Thank you for just being you
When everyone else was false towards me
You were true
But I knew that
We would have to move on
That whatever we had
Would be gone
I'm not saying it was wrong
It just wasn't meant to
Last that long
Like a one hit wonder
Type of song
We were just two people going
In different directions
That happened to meet while crossing

The intersection
Now we're going
To different
Schools this august
And to be honest
I'll miss you
But I truly
Wish you the best of luck
With whatever you do
Life is made up of beautiful
Short yet priceless moments
And for me
You were one of those moments

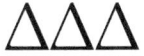

China Town

Fell out of heaven
On the
Elevator floor eleven
Saw my sins
My losses and wins
Creatures call for me
Saying I must pay
The heaviest fee
The mind says stay
The heart says flee
I cried that day
Only moonlight
No sunray
I bow to the crowd
Their cheers are loud
For a second
I feel proud
Motionless I stand
Within this mysterious
Land
Full of dragons
Tigers
Nothing seems the same
Here
Yet I feel no fear

Now fighting snakes
With this golden spear
This must be a dream
Since it would seem
I was pure
A beam of light
A hero defeating the night
This power feels so
Right
As
I vanquish evil
With one strike
Of this vengeful might

ΔΔΔ

The Fortune

You are loved
You are wanted
You are unique
You are at your
Peak
You know how
To truly
Speak
You are the
Opposite
Of weak
You are the
Creator
Of
Your own
Fate
You cannot wait
For anyone
Or else
It
Will be too
Late
You're working
Hard
That's great

But
You need to
Work harder
From when the
Sun rises
To when
It falls
And through
Time
While the moon
Calls
This is your time
Pick up that
Lucky dime
Reverse the curse
Add to this earth
Your own personal
Verse

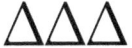

The Question

Crowds
Of millions
Gather
To ask
To unmask
This simple
Question
This worldwide
Depression
This ambitious
Progression
This sinner's
Confession
This band's
Jam session
This artist's
Expression
This theater's
Concession
This teacher's
Profession
This first date's
Impression
This scientist's
Obsession

Oh so many
Questions
To be heard
All surrounding
Ten words
How did I
Get here
And
Who created
The birds?

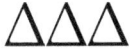

The Answer

Two plus two
Red roses
Violets
Are sometimes
Blue
Light flashes
That's our
Cue
To answer
Them
But only if
We really knew
Why the roses
Are red
Or
What they really
Said
Or if Elvis
Is really
Dead
Or
How we got here
Who created
Fear
Why we all

Have to have
A career
I guess in
The end
It just
Depends
On who you've
Become
Doesn't matter what
The past has
Done
Just matters
Who you are
Under this
Bright yellow sun

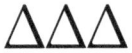

Underwater Graveyard

Moss growing
East
Seaweed
Feeding the
Beast
Temples searching
For a
Priest
Coral looking
For a new
Reef
These tears
Puddle into
Grief
Everyday
We're turning
A new leaf
Cold liquid
Surrounds
These
Watery grounds
These
Unspoken
Towns
These

Empty hills
With
Fervent sounds
Sacred stones
Weighing more
Than
Ten million
Pounds
Curious ghosts
Move swiftly
Upon these
Grounds

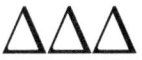

Just Passing By

There once was a man
Named Time
Now
Everyday he would
Walk past the bus stop
And with each day
He would notice a young man
No older than twenty
Sitting there
Telling people of his
Grand and lavish plans
To become rich and famous
Everyone believed in him
1, 3, 7, 18 years washed away
And the once young man
Was now a middle-aged man
Sitting on the same bench
Heading to the same job
The man named Time
Watched as the now half-life man
Spoke of his future
Goals and dreams
The man named
Time
Shook his head

Solemn faced
And walked away
20, 28, 45 more years
Float away
The once middle-aged
Yet now
83 year-old man
Sitting on the same bench
Waiting for another bus
Speaking of his future as if he'll live forever
The man named Time
Noticed the old man's eyes
Watching him
"Hey, I've seen you everyday for the past 63 years
Walking by this bus stop...who are you?"
Said the old man
Time simply stared and gave a reply
"Oh don't mind me, I'm just passing by"

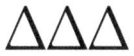

The Thoughts I Have At Midnight

Still awake
Thinking about my failures
Poetic genius we all are
I guess any bright light
Could be a shooting star
My rhymes
Are still up to par
Scoop a spoonful
Out of this honey jar
Throw the cigarette
Out of my car
Everything seems quiet
Yet my mind
Is starting a riot
Hours passing by
Testing this hypothesis
Asking why
Certain people live
And why others die
3 in the morning mist
Wondering if I'll make
It onto the eternal list
2 choices

And a
Tattoo on my wrist
Don't look at me
The mirror hit my fist
I wish it wasn't you
That I kissed
Ah screw it
Who's actually reading this

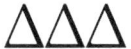

Villain

Sitting in this lecture
Being taught by some guy named
Hannibal lecter
He invited me over for dinner
Saying I'm a winner
Got the highest grade on the test
To be honest
I cheated off that one girl
The wicked witch of the west
But I'm the
Good guy
I
Could never kill
Or lie
Unless I was
The Anti
Hero
Like Godzilla
Or that
Huge Gorilla
These rhymes stay cold
'Cause I keep it vanilla
Swords in the hand
Of Attila The Hun
These Jokers

Choosing knives
Over a gun
If you're not a cop
Then you should run
I'm not evil
Yet I wrote this for fun
Tripped the waiter
Holding that Luke warm water
For some guy named Vader
Here's a cheat code for
The game of life we're all in
7 letters
Villain

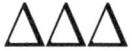

Gods And Monsters

Life is the elusive
Mysterious creature
Who tries to convert
The preacher
The ghoul that outsmarts
The teacher
Pitch black box
Watching this double feature
Prayed 45 times today
Been doing this since May 10th
Saw Dracula hop the fence
While trying to free
The mummy
From his sarcophagus
Slept in early
Missed the bus
We seek guidance
Within the darkness
Descending into the abyss
We are driven by flames
And calmed by the mist
In the end, what will be the twist
The conclusion
To who
Created mankind's fist

Seeking the unknown
Pushing away the known
We stand here
Upon this stone
On the outside we are brave
Yet inside, we are truly alone

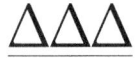

It's Us Versus Them

So here's the analogy
Using this strategy
Coming against
Common Neutrality
We all have dreams
So what's yours
You know
That quiet thought
That they tell us not
To believe in or pursue
Yet we keep thinking about it
Don't you ever want to capitalize
On that inner fire
The desire to overcome
These obstacles
Blocking our way out
Of this prison
Now please listen
The ones seeking fame
Will forget their own name

The ones who easily fold
Will fall for copper
When they could be getting gold
I'll be waiting for the moment
When I accept this gem
For today, tomorrow, and forever
It's us versus them

ΔΔΔ

———————

You

Nights like these
Middle of the night breeze
Like regrets dripping from trees
That moment
I was supposed to seize
My feelings still unclear
The future is full of fear
The past will always last
Inside my heart
According to the chart
I may have missed my chance
From the start
Like a dart
Missing the bullseye
Yet here I am asking why
Didn't I try
hard enough
Did I say
The wrong stuff
I smiled

And you called my bluff
I've only felt this way
For a few
If only you knew
How I feel for you

Volume 3

From Success

We learn so much more from failure
Than we ever could from success
Realize you're blessed
And begin on the quest
To see what you knew
This whole time

Been paying my due

Call this an artistic crime
But if I were you
I'd choose the cherry over the lime
Drinks and Herbs around all the time
Consume this culture
Nothing against it
I see it as a nice fit
To distract us from ever knowing
We could ever quit
At any second, any minute
Yet I was born for this
To win it

Live The Moment

The past can feel so close
And the future
The future can feel as if it's about to happen
But the present
The present is here
Now for us
For us to live the moment

New Places

Sit back and drift away
Float onto some other day
Time machine
August back to May
But I'll choose to stay
Here with you

If fear pushed you down
What would you do
Stay defeated
Or stand back up

Wipe the dirt off
And say enough is enough
Take back your dreams
Dreams so big
They could reach the farthest planet
That gleams
Off in the distance
Are you willing to go the distance
That it will take to win
These races
That'll take us to new places

Shall We Destroy

Appreciate everything
Even the cold nights
For they make the warm days
Feel even warmer

And hate
Let go of hate
For it serves no purpose
But to destroy

And love
Give, show, and experience love
With everyone you can
For if we can let go of hate
And replace it with love

Then and only then
Shall we destroy fear

So I Say

I cannot say this enough
People will try and tear you down
They will tell you
You are not strong enough
They'll pull you down to their level
And say it's impossible

So I say
Never
Ever

And I mean never
Let anyone bring you down

Strong Winds On A Gloomy Day

The gust
Came from the west
Sweatpants and a light blue vest
I wore that day
You wore a sundress
The color of May
I asked if you would stay
That if there was any way
To change your mind
And that we could still wind
Up together
Sometime within forever
But you closed your eyes
And softly said never
Could we ever be together
Sometime within any forever
In that moment
Near my heart
I pulled a lever
Drifted up into the sky
As light as a feather
Facing all fear
Pushing against this gloomy weather

Sunday Poem

In the Wild Wild West
I think I said it best
All day I write
From when the sun is born
To when it dies at night
We are the children of light
Born to fight, the good fight
Climbing this skyscraper
Reaching a new height
No goal is ever outta sight
19 years ago I reacted
And was created
Devil and God
Sat there and debated
Whether I'd be loved or hated
Luckily for common sense
I hopped the fence
And found a forest
That was quite dense
Started playing with the idea
Creativity could never be limited
So that's exactly what I did
Opened Pandora's box
And destroyed the lid
I was the strongest kid
Then Lady Luck
Placed the highest bid on my soul
Ever since then
Life has been out of my control

Pure

This feeling came out of nowhere
Striking my heart and soul
All at once
I never had the chance to understand it
Only the short amount of time
To accept it
To learn to live with it

Is You

You believe perfection is everything
But you don't know
That I love the way you smile
And that little laugh of yours
How you take time to think
Or the way your eyes open
When you're surprised
You believe perfection is everything
Yet I believe perfection
Is you

Society Told Me So

Indifference looked it up
Then wasn't interested, kids these days
All focused on what others did
Yesterday, like did that girl
Text me hey
Did they leave the party or stay
Do they follow me on insta
Or like me in any way
Blah blah blah
Something about someone named bae
Part of this generation
That grew up in a day
But you see
That's who society tells me to be
But that's not for me
I like to travel the trail
That leads me to a key
To build and open the door
That'll align me with the stars
'Cause I like to make birdies
More than pars
But most kids these days
Get stuck in bars
Focusing on gossip
And dreaming of exotic cars
So you do you
I'll keep working till I reach Mars

To Treat Her Right

Yes I talk about love
In almost every piece I write
Not just poetry
But in the stories I tell myself at night
Of why we couldn't make it work
Or how If I hadn't rushed
Everything would be different
That I'd still be there for you
I guess what I mean
Is I talk about love a lot
As If I feel it constantly
But the truth I face
Is that it's something
I'm working towards
To find that person
And treat her right
To take care of her and show her
How much she means to me

That's what I'm feeling right now

Then, Now, and Forever

She smiled,
As he held her close
So that neither
The past
Nor future could hurt her
She guarded him from the present
Frozen they sat
Within forever

Million Years

She asked,
If he would ever leave
He smiled
As he gently held her hand
She smiled as he
Softly moved the hair from in front of her eyes
And replied
If I did, who would be here to hold your hand

Lonely Little Star

Stuck in this midnight dream
Voice quiet
But the heart is about to scream
Empty house, Empty house
Lonely man, lonely man
Thinking of you
Yet I know not who you are
Maybe love just hasn't drifted
It's way towards my
Lonely little star

Two

The stars
Were made for two
Two souls
Holding onto
Each other, to never
Let go
Never

Restart

It was the idea
That stuck itself
Within the cracks of his mind
The idea
That maybe one day
He would be
In some other place
With some other person
To start over
Once again

The Fame

In the middle of the night
It was never the fame
Nor
The money
Nor
The power that he dreamed of
It was her eyes
The eyes he had fallen for
Time after time

Regret

Within minutes
The regret could be felt
Growing within him
Like a gremlin
Who never wanted
The good guy to win
His previous sin
Consumed his thoughts
Pushed him against the rocks
Made him watch the wax
Drip from the candle lit clocks

The Here and Now

Choose to notice
The little things
That occurs around us everyday
Watch as the birds
Soar amongst the blue sky
Listen to the laughter
That happens everyday
The sound of pure happiness
The past is gone
The future has not yet been defined
But the present
Has been formed uniquely
Just for you

Your Forever

Life's too short
To not be passionate
Life's too short
To not live in the moment
Life's too short
To be afraid of taking chances
Life's too short
To care what they think
Life's too short
To think you could never do something
Life's too short
To let the waves crash down
And beat you
So stand up and run towards
Your forever

Hollow

Notorious at first
These hollow dungeons are cursed
We ignore the best
And focus on the worst
Beginning at an unknown date
Using human emotions
As some sort of bait
Years went by
Slow motion type of rate
Rusty metal formed as it's gate
10, 20, 30
Years or at some later date
A light turns on
And awaiting is a crate
Too soon or yet again
Too late
It has chosen
Now
To reveal its fate

August Made Me Realize

31 days
Of warm summer air
Upon time where each shall dare
To adventure out there
Inside the old summer air
Underneath the warm
Summer glare
Beware and be aware
That things will be easy
And
Things will be tough
No sea captain
Has ever ventured into seas
That may never become rough
The true difference
Between the ones that make it
And the ones that do not
Is that when the going gets tough
They will never stop
They will sow their ideas
And reap from their crop
Success is subjective

Then again
So are other's thoughts

Never

Life said quit

...

The heart then laughed
And
Replied saying
Never

Green Striped Door

Stood near the edge
And jumped towards my dream
Fell into a nearby stream
It washed me onto the shore
Of things that are no more
I stood up
Walked a few feet
And noticed a door
It was red with green stripes
And around the edges
Were flickering neon lights
That lit up the sky
During these gloomy nights

Missed Something

Do you ever feel
As if there was a certain
Moment
Back then
Where you missed something
An important moment
Where if you had acted differently
Or
Had said the right thing
That everything would be different
For better or for worse
Things would at least be different

Smile For No Reason

Life is fast
Ever moving
Never ceasing
To exist
Seconds move
Minutes roll on
Years tick by
So love the ones
Closest to you
Kiss passionately
Hold onto the moment
For as long as you possibly can
Seize the day
Remain calm
While the rest of the world yells
Laugh forever
Notice the small things
And
Smile for absolutely no reason

S l o w M o t i o n

Everyone
Has somewhere to be
Someone else to see
Always rushing to the next thing
Focusing on the future
While unknowingly living
In the present moment
Most of us think
That once we get to that "place"
That infamous "place" of endless happiness
In our lives
That we'll be content, happy,
&
Finally able to live a fulfilling life
Yet if that were true
What are we doing right now
Laughing, loving, and living
You see the sad but honest truth
Is that we should be less focused
On the destination of our life
And more on the
Journey of life
You see the adventure
We are all on
The adventure of reaching
Our destination

Is without a doubt
Life itself

Till I Saw

This feeling is of fear
Not the natural kind of fear
It's the fear which resides deep within
The one that wants me to fail
Not win
Next to doubt
The one that reminds me
That these dreams could collapse any second
The one that tells me
I may not be good enough
This is the feeling that resided
Till I saw the obstacle
And beat it
Till I faced the obstacle
And beat it

The Realize

We are born
In one day
We die
In one day
Life moves around
As we walk towards the finish line
Notice everything
Experience and trust
Love and honor
Yourself as you live life

Took Away

This thought erases my memories
Taking away the bad with the good
These feelings are all I have left
If I should let
These feelings keep me up at night
Whether it's
Wrong or right
My heart will battle the mind
In this ongoing fight
Nothing is ever just
Black & White
Things are not how they appear
These feelings took away my courage
And replaced it
With fear

For Now

For now
We are young
Free
To make mistakes
Free
To fall in love
Free
To laugh & be silly
Free
To smile while the thunder roars
Free
To live
Because for now
We are young

This Is Your Life

I honestly think it's
Completely & utterly ridiculous
When people are too afraid
To go after what they love to do
Just because they feel as if someone has to
Tell them it's finally ok to chase their dreams
Like seriously, this is your life
No one is going to tell you when
To go after that goal of yours
You need to decide
That for yourself
Do what makes you the happiest
Because
It doesn't matter what these
Other
People think

Dusty Planet

We fell from the heavens
And built our home
Here on this dusty planet
Creating the language
Needed to bring us together
We formed a culture
That society took advantage of

I Believe

I believe happiness
Is achieved
When you are fully content
With what you have
And not
With what you want

Because They Felt

I think it's cool
When people just do things
When they don't stop
And waste an hour
Wondering what people will think
Or how many likes it'll get them
They just do it because
They wanted to
Because they felt like doing it

That's cool

The Life We Lived

In the end
I hope you realize
That in life, there won't be this
Grand moment where the universe
Finally makes sense
And
Things are perfect
But that life
Had been made up
Of short yet beautifully
Unique moments
That collected together
And created
The life we lived

To Look At Fear

Strength has never been
The ability
To smile when things
Are perfect
But has been the ability to truly find
Who you are
In the most fearful circumstances
The chance to look at fear
One on one
And decide how you will act
At your lowest
To have the strength
To look at fear

Ever Forward

Do what you love
Forget the worries
Let them go
Each day is a fresh start
A chance to regain focus
To move forward
Ever forward

To Tell The World

Within the act of creation
Comes the adventure of discovery
The chance to find new light
In an ordinary world
The chance to leave your mark
On this earth to tell the world
You were here
You lived
&
Breathed this fresh open air
So many will hide
Only few shall dare
To find who they truly are
Within this fresh open air

Fell From Heaven

I contemplate each night
If what I do is right
Forgetting the past
Hoping each second will last
Longer than 10 years combined
I tried & tried
Fell from heaven, but never cried
I'm not perfect
But this much is true
I fell in love once
And didn't even have a clue
It was you

Softly Said,

Almost there
His consciousness told the heart
The heart was tired and afraid
But the essence
And idea that drove
His soul to believe
In the impossible
Softly said,
In the moments
We feel afraid, low, and dismayed
Never let go
Never let those dreams fade

Could Never Be

Thought about it
Really did
I've believed in something
Greater since I was a kid
The letters
That formed my life
These words
I have begun to type
Introduces a man to me
I thought I could never be

Own Ways

What we once had
Was beautiful
Simple in fact
And though we have
Gone our own ways
There's no reason
Not to smile
When thinking of then

Who You Are

People talk
They always will
You just need to know
Who you are
&
Where you're going
And you'll be just fine

Everything You Got

If you're going to go after something
And I mean really go after it
Not just say you will
In a few years
Like everyone else
Then hell
Go after it with
Everything you got kid

Red & White Potions

You criticize
Practically demoralize
The future ideas
That came to me in a dream
After I inhaled this potions
Red & white steam
Into my lungs it fell
Like rain water scurrying down a well
I'm in heaven
But maybe this is hell
Yet it's too soon
Too hard to tell

Fell A Little

Again I saw
That whenever
I thought of us
I fell a little harder
For you

This In Person

I was afraid
Honestly was
Always been afraid
Of being alone
But ever since you
Came around these thoughts aren't as heavy
These letters feel softer
Wish I could say this in person
But these words
Are all I have

Skin & Bones

You can choose
To feel afraid
To see your dream fade
Or you can
Strive into the unknown
With the skin
On your back
And the strength in your bone

- Volume 1, Uno (2014)

What You See

All it takes is belief
In fact
It only takes
You to believe in it
No one else
Needs to see the vision
If they do
Then great
If they don't
That's perfectly fine
It's what you see
That makes your dreams happen
3, 2, 1
Close my eyes
And believe

That's all it takes

Be You

Take a chance tonight
Smile bigger than ever
Ask that person out
Laugh too much
Be silly
Completely forgive others
Live life fully in the moment
Never look back
And above all else
Be you

When They Can

I truly without
Any doubt believe
That it's unbelievably beautiful
When people are themselves
When they can
Walk into the world
And say
This is who I am
Love me or hate me
This is who I am

The Way You Went

I don't remember
Falling for you
I only recall
Fearing the moment
In which I'd have
To let you go

The Only

The only way
To go far
Is to lose sight
Of what you know

Reflection

For the longest
Time I believed
You looked at me
The same way
But realized too late
It was the reflection
From my own eyes

Magic We Call Time

Time has always been part magic
Part a trick
Yeah it's helpful if you
Need to meet somewhere
At a certain moment
Yet if you truly think about it
The future only lives
In our minds
While the past survives
In our minds as well
The present moment is the only real concept
That gives us the choice
To live in the moment
Allowing us the chance to let go
Of both
The

Past and future

This magic we call time
This trick we call time
Has been created to only distract us
From living in the now

Once Again

The stars hung
Far away from the earth
Hoping that one day
They'd be able
To see their old friend
Once again

In Life

The truth is
That in life the worst thing
You'll have to face
In order to
Achieve those dreams of yours
Is simply yourself

Others

The true difference
Between the ones who make it
And the ones who do not
Is that when the going gets tough
They will never stop
They will sow their ideas
And reap from their crop
Success is subjective
Then again
So are other's thoughts

(Repeated knowledge)

Yet nonetheless important

Fail Brilliantly

And if you must fail my child
Fail brilliantly
So that once you succeed
You will truly
Know the difference

Jump

Sometimes you need
To just go for it
And jump
Into the unknown
Praying you'll land
In the right place
With the right person
In the right moment

Believed

I believed in something
Greater than myself
I believed in something
To believe again

I Truly Hope

I truly hope you're happy
That he…
That wherever you are
That you're so incredibly happy
That you still smile the same way
And laugh even if nobody else is
That you still watch
As the
Sun & moon
Pass by eachother
As one descends
&
The other rises
And poetry
I hope you still love poetry

I fell in love once.

⇧
o

In The End

It drove me away
Then pulled me back
From what I would gain
I would find what I lacked
This bridge was already burning
Before it had cracked
My only hope
My only wish
Is in the end
You never forget our kiss

Her Eyes

In the end
All he truly needed
Was to look
Into her eyes
Once again

Seventeen Words

Get lost in those
Dreams of yours kid
This world already
Has enough people
Who say no

Best seventeen words I ever heard

Thinking

I sometimes believe
That I'm the last
Person on earth
Forced to walk alone forever

Thinking of the day
I'd maybe
Run into you

So Cold

I could feel the wind
On my back that day
As you walked away
It was pushing us apart
From the start
I believed you deserved
To have and hold
My heart
Or so I was told
It was warmer with you
Yet now the air feels so cold

Even When

Even when I close
My eyes
And count to 10
I still see you
Even when I pray
For our memories
To evaporate
I still remember you
Even when I hope
To have moved on
I still miss you

If You Must Ask

And if you must ask
Success cannot be defined
By
Fame or money
Success is defined
By
The completion of doing
What you love to do

Volume 4

(THE FINAL VOLUME)

The Flare

I stood there
Staring straight up
In the air
Looking at the flare
It looked back at me
Must have been shot off
Near the county fair
I should have told you
That I care
You were someone
That turned out to be so rare
I just didn't have time
To prepare
What my emotions would feel
In the end
Let's make a deal
My love for you
Could break through steel
I'd let it all go
But success is at the edge
Of my heel

Contrary To Unpopular Belief

The scientist told the people
That life is out there
That if you look close enough
You can still see them
The bright lights of the past
That shines & sparkles
Just for us
We are the future
Yet at the same time
We are the present
Our job is to make sure we get home safely
So that we can safely hand
The next generation the torch
The torch in which we created
Whether made of bad or good choices
It still lights
And the fire rises within the chosen few
Who decide
To go farther and become something new

It Takes Time

The idea spun me around
The power of the sound
Took me somewhere
I thought would never be found
The drive
The fire
The determination
Call it what you will
But my creativity
Just can't sit still
Good thing
This was all a blessing
Not a curse
Not something
That could make matters worse

To My Generation

To my generation
Let us shape the world
Let our voices be heard
Run fast
Jump high
Break every barrier
Those adults ever put in the sky
I hope you give it everything
I hope you give it a try
We all know the truth
Taking action is deep
Talking about it
Is straight up cheap
So be real
Let the world know
How you really feel

Romance & Death

The two
Romance & Death
Danced like old friends
Made their peace
Said their amends
I've danced with both
Chill herb
Rolling down that PCH coast
If I had given up
My dreams would be toast
Burnt to a crisp
Cooked to a roast
I delight in failure
Success might as well be a stranger
But anyways I'm off
To beat some more danger

Between Those Thoughts

Growing up can be
Crazy, wonderful, terrifying, exhilarating
All at the same time
It can hit you when you're not looking
And carry you when you need it most
In the end, trust your instincts
And do what you love
For I believe
Happiness
Rests somewhere between those thoughts

The World I Was Placed In

The dust & gravel
Settle down & unravel
Before my eyes
Stood pure blue skies
On the tip of our tongues
Rests pretty white lies
Once you've felt the lows
You'll search for the highs
True beauty is unseen
As it rests in its disguise
The world I was placed in
Was built for the wise,
The go-getters, doers,
And for the man who tries
Nothing ever comes easy
My father told me
You have to take it
Push harder than ever
Truly make it or break it
Because
The world we were all placed in
Is a place
Where we have to fight to win

Prayer

The most well known
The most overlooked
The most needed
The most controversial
The most challenging
Thing I can think of
Is prayer
How most of us see no point to it
Belief aside
Prayer is something unique
A moment to take a break
Close our eyes
&
Slow down
To let go of fear
To return some needed hope
To feel loved
To feel meaning

The Fall

Kings rise
Conquer cities unknown
Take what they want
And move on
Yet no palace is forever
No kingdom is everlasting
No royalty is infinite
They all fall
They all become human
After the lights go out
&
The world moves past the
Temporary power
As it
Relies heavily on the present moment
As does life
We have now
To rule, discover, and reach great heights
The future does not exist
&
The past is buried within our memories
We have now
We have the time to live
Before the fall

For A Few

Fell for a few
Thought I knew what to do
Played the game
Too many times
I sat puzzled
Yet inspired to resurrect these new rhymes
Between you and I
I'm just a man
Who decided to stay
And never ran
Learning from wrong & right
Our culture teaches us to be tough
Look the other way
And back down from a fight
Yet I stay feeling rough
Continuously calling their bluff
Shooting for the stars
While I try to buy momma & sis
Brand new cars
I got dreams
I got aspirations
And no one
Will ever stand in the way of that determination

Reoccurring

Thought I'd write to you again
Give it all I got
Speak like a real man
Stand up straight
With nostalgia in each hand
Times are happening
People are changing
My life
Is literally rearranging
And I've never been a poet
Just a writer
Who poetically shows it

These Wonders

These wonders
These thoughts
Stimulate my mind
Ask some questions
Then leave me blind
Everything is relative
People these days are so sensitive
Yet maybe that's good
Since I'm trying to stand
Where the greats stood
Everyday we change
Always remember that
Everyday we try on a new hat
Sit down where our
Ancestors sat
Then gain the courage
To beat our demons with a bat
It takes belief to go far
To pass the moon
And discover a new star
To run faster than a speeding car
We preach but never practice
What we've been taught
We forget we are only a dot
On this planet

Push Away

Away
Above
Around
Push, pull, and melt
This physical body of sound
I feel lost
But I just found
Out
That there's another route
Towards what I want
To what I need
Got the water
Plant the seed
Let it sprout up
Into a magnificent tree
Then you'll see what I see
Or what I've seen
All these years
Passed me by
Not going to lie
I'm the good guy
So stay
While I push away

New York, 2013

On the flight
That stormy November night
I recall a feeling
That I was currently dealing
With
My trip was from
The 15th to the 25th
About ten days
In the city that resembles a maze
I remember the fog
It resembled the herbs haze
The sidewalk felt tougher
The language felt rougher
The world I knew
Had been split in two
So what was a young man to do
He was to grow up
Drink for the first time
And throw up
A metaphor of course
Nonetheless I became a man
Learned how to stand
I was a young scout
Returning to his promise land
And there I stood
The moon couldn't shine any brighter
Squeezing my fist tighter
My passion and drive
Was hotter than any lighter
Because there
I became a writer

Brand New Ideas

The last one
After this I'm done
With poetry at least
This feels unreal
This feels like
My dreams are now deceased
Or maybe the dream
Has just been increased
Maybe I'm thinking bigger now
But how
Could a kid like me
Gain the courage to face a world like thee
Stories I'll tell explore cities
Deep down under the sea
But between you and me
I still have so much more
So much in store
So if you're joining us now on this tour
Thank you
Sit down
Buckle up
Get your clocks set
Because
You ain't seen nothing yet

www.ingramcontent.com/pod-product-compliance
Lightning Source LLC
Chambersburg PA
CBHW051458170526
45166CB00001B/296